Solitude in Serendipity:

Solo Journeys in Sri Lanka

While every precaution has been taken in the preparation of this book, the publisher assumes no responsibility for errors or omissions, or for damages resulting from the use of the information contained herein.

SOLITUDE IN SERENDIPITY: SOLO JOURNEYS IN SRI LANKA

First edition. May 9, 2024.

ISBN: 979-8224275748

Written by Chetan Dhumane and Joy Bose.

Table of Contents

Dedication

This book is dedicated to friendship between India and Sri Lanka and between the people of India and Sri Lanka.

Acknowledgements

The authors are grateful to multiple people for making this book possible.

In particular, Chetan would like to thank his parents and friends, whose unwavering love and support have been the cornerstone of his journey.He would also like to express gratitude to the countless tour guides whose knowledge and passion enriched his journey with unforgettable experiences and insights.

Joy would like to thank his tour guide Pala during his journey in Sri Lanka.

Introduction

This book is an account of solo journeys to Sri Lanka by the two authors.

Chetan visited Sri Lanka in December 2023, and experienced its amazing food, culture and in particular the tea and coffee plantations.

Joy visited Sri Lanka a few times between 2015 and 2021, mainly for exploring the Buddhist and other archeological heritage of Sri Lanka in what is called the cultural triangle, consisting of Anuradhapura, Polonnaruwa, Dambulla and Kandy.

PART 1: Chetan's Journeys in Sri Lanka

Chapter 1: Prologue

Hello All , welcome to my second book on my trip to Sri lanka. This travel journey was my first international trip . If you want to visit Sri Lanka from India, this book can act as your small guide .

I decided to visit Sri lanka as a solo traveler because I wanted to avoid the unwanted noise and distraction which appears when we travel in a group. Many disagreements would happen over place selection , events selection and travel plans.

So this book is for you , if you want to travel as a solo traveler from India. If you are traveling from other countries that would also help.

I dont travel anywhere on a target basis like increasing the number of spots to visit in 2 days etc.

Instead this book is for the people who are open minded and can visit any place which comes within the journey time and place .

As per my understanding when a person travels as a solo traveler the person should be able to explore culture , local markets and talk to people of the particular country/place , should have an open conversation with local people and culture.

My first book was on my coffee journey towards Bangalore .

I will be trying to cover which places I was able to cover in my 6-7 days of journey to Sri Lanka from Pune, India.

You can make your own journey. This book can help you decide on some factors.

Chapter 2: How it all started

———

Friend of mine just visited Sri lanka last year , it all started in my mind to visit this country when my friend came back from Sri lanka. He gave me some local taxi contacts, to begin with my journey.

I started searching a lot on travel within Sri lanka for my stay . I found out we can travel within Sri Lanka easily by train for a longer distance with low cost. You just have to book all your journey in advance from the website.

Website Link for train bookings : https://seatreservation.railway.gov.lk/mtktwebslr/

You can easily book your home stays using agoda. While booking the home stays please check all reviews on google maps , there should be many review counts by foreigners who stayed there , count should not be less than 50 .

If you are a solo traveler Homestays are better otherwise you can book 3-star or 5 -star hotels too as per your convenience.

You have to check all ratings on agoda before booking it on agoda and also check for all refund policies before you book your rooms .

I would say first you should book all your train tickets on priority , then book for your flight tickets.

To save on costs , you can book your flight tickets from Chennai to Colombo.

Train timetable help website

https://colombofort.com/train.schedule.htm

Source : http://www.railway.gov.lk/

Once you book the train ticket online , remember to take the physical print out of the ticket from the train station . You can show your copy of the E ticket and take the print while traveling.

Other modes of transport Like Uber and Pick Me work in urban areas not within villages. You have to make sure you have enough contacts of Trusted cab drivers.

Network :

Get the local SIM Card preferably **Dialog 4G** on another phone to use as Hotspot.

Banking :

Use of **Bank Ceylon ATM preferably** to withdraw the cash in LKR. I prefer this bank as the conversion charges were very less for Indian debit cards.

You can also do currency exchange once you arrive at Colombo international airport if you have Indian currency with you.

Most of the shops and restaurants will accept the cards , in villages this facility may not be there. So always prefer to have cash with you.

Compare the currency rate , inflation and all factors .

Always remember if you are a SAARC citizen you can get special discounts on some spots like museums etc. You may have to show your passport to the officer and confirm at the place before buying any ticket. Check the wikipedia page to see if you are a SAARC member or not.

Contact Details

Cab Help Darshan : + 94 722500380

Hugging Clouds Guest House Near Adams Peak : +94 721826333

COCO House/Rooms Near Galle : +94 766807636

Suwani Pinnawala Homestay : this is near Elephant Orphanage at Pinnawala

Village Restaurant near Gampola

Chapter 3: Day 1 in Colombo

When I arrived at Colombo using Fits Air using Chennai to Colombo Flight on 25th December , I contacted Darshan to take me to the hotel where I booked my one day stay at the Grand Oriental Hotel. I chose this hotel as it was very near to Colombo train station and nearby to many famous places.

When I landed at Colombo Airport , I was advised by Shereen to get the Dialog SIM Card.

I took the Dialog SIM card and activated it on another phone and started using the 4G network using wifi hotspot.

I wanted to explore the coffee culture in Sri Lanka , I understood that Tea culture is more active in Sri Lanka as of now . But still I went to the Java Lounge near my hotel.

This cafe is very famous within Colombo and you can get here easily from this hotel. During the walk I saw many lottery retailers selling lotteries. Lottery style was very fancy. I took some for the collection.

When I entered the Java Lounge I inquired about coffee origin. I understood they use the Starbucks sourced coffees so I took Americano and it tasted very nice.

Grand Oriental Hotel Colombo Entrance Lobby

A grand entrance featuring elegant decor, luxurious furnishings, and welcoming ambiance, setting the tone for a memorable stay.

Hotel Room in Grand Oriental Hotel , Colombo

The bed in the image is a four-poster bed with a canopy. The frame is made of dark wood, possibly mahogany or walnut. The canopy fabric is white and appears to be made of a sheer or voile material. There are two white pillows on the bed and a white sheet. The headboard has a rounded top and the bedposts are square with decorative details at the top. This style of bed is often called a tester bed and can add a touch of luxury.

View from the Grand Oriental Hotel Colombo Buffet Place.

The Grand Oriental Hotel lunch room offers a panoramic view of the bustling Port of Colombo, where massive ships glide by as you dine. It's a captivating sight, enhancing your meal with the vibrant energy of maritime commerce right outside the window.

Java Lounge in Colombo

Look no further than Java Lounge, a popular chain of cafes and restaurants known for their inviting atmosphere and delicious offerings. They go beyond just coffee, boasting a diverse menu of snacks and meals, perfect for a relaxing breakfast, lunch, or casual dinner. Whether you're a local or a tourist, Java Lounge provides a cozy and modern space to unwind and savor a delightful dining experience.

Taking a coffee here is a blissful experience after your arrival :)

In the background, you can see a view of a harbor. There are large cargo ships docked at the piers, and smaller boats can be seen moving in the water.Enjoy your cup of coffee with this great view of the port of colombo.

So this was the a la carte menu item . Rice was really delicious with egg spread on it.

I have also started roaming on the streets of Colombo , I was amazed to see the cleanliness of the roads and there were no traffic jams , not much traffic as well.

There are trees lining the street with colorful tuk-tuks parked in front of them. People mill about on the sidewalks, some carrying shopping bags.In the background, there is a large white building with a clock tower.There are also other colonial-era buildings lining the street. The sky is a clear blue.

Some road in colombo , Lined with charming old buildings in rustic white and brown hues, evoking a nostalgic charm amidst the bustling cityscape.

This picture I took when I was around **Java Lounge in Colombo .**

I started searching on google for the great places to visit nearby so after taking my caffeine intake at Java Lounge I have decided to visit **Gangarama Maha Vihara Temple** , my initial plan was to visit **One Galle Face Mall** , but when I took uber I went near the mall , I saw huge queue of the people then I guided Uber driver to visit the temple instead of One Galle Face Mall .

I found that my decision was perfect as per the condition of that day. I truly enjoyed the atmosphere of the temple , and was able to meditate in the temple for sometime. I will encourage you to visit this temple and spend some time here. Please follow all temple Rules.

I saw there are many old collections in the temple converted into a museum which you can truly enjoy if you love history and ancient times.

I will share the pictures of the same here.

A serene photo capturing the essence of Buddhism: A majestic Buddha statue radiates tranquility, surrounded by offerings, and intricate Buddha faces.

Wood-carved serenity: A meditative man depicted in intricate woodwork, embodying peace and mindfulness, inviting contemplation and inner reflection.

Inside this temple there is very nice architecture. Just like you see in the image , Lord Gautam Buddha statues are present in the queue format on every row. You will be very peaceful and calm once you enter this temple and start looking at different architecture types.

Lord Ganesh, revered in Hinduism, symbolizes wisdom, prosperity, and remover of obstacles, depicted with an elephant head and a potbelly.I found this art very unique. You can see the color of this frame , placement of the flowers and sitting posture of Lord ganesha.

Amidst the serene ambiance of Gangaramaya Temple, Gautam Buddha sits in tranquil contemplation. The air resonates with profound spirituality, enveloping the surroundings in a gentle embrace. His presence infuses the temple with a timeless wisdom, inviting seekers to immerse themselves in the stillness of his enlightened aura.

When you come out of the temple , you can observe this machine .

I wanted to see Independence Square too but it was already evening :(, tomorrow morning I had a train booking for Hatton and I have decided to have a look at Independence Square even if it is evening.

This is the picture I captured while traveling using Uber .

The above red tower known as Lotus tower will be visible to you across Colombo city . You can visit this tower by paying some visiting amount , first check if you have any discounts if you are a SAARC citizen.

The Lotus Tower in Colombo, Sri Lanka, stands as a symbol of national pride and technological advancement. This towering structure, resembling a blooming lotus flower, serves as a telecommunications and observation tower, offering panoramic views of the city while showcasing Sri Lanka's modern architectural prowess to the world.

Independence Square area at night .

At Independence Square in Colombo, the night unveils a captivating scene. Illuminated pathways guide strollers past tranquil ponds and statues, while the grand Independence Memorial Hall stands as a beacon of national heritage. The ambiance is serene, with soft lighting creating an enchanting atmosphere for reflection and leisurely walks.

Independence Square area at night .

I had my dinner inside Independence Square that night and started towards my Hotel at Grand Oriental Hotel .

Cargills store on the night of 25th December .

Cargills, a leading supermarket chain in Sri Lanka, offers a diverse array of groceries, fresh produce, and household items. Its stores provide a convenient shopping experience with quality products at affordable prices. With a focus on customer satisfaction and innovation, Cargills continues to be a beloved choice for shoppers nationwide.

When I came back to the hotel after a big day's journey , I saw the below given board inside the Grand Oriental Hotel.

The **Grand Oriental Hotel in Colombo**, Sri Lanka, established in 1837, holds a rich history as a colonial-era landmark and premier hospitality destination.

This hotel has a great history. I was amazed and felt proud that many great people lived here .

As you walk near your room in the hotel , you can see great old paintings hanging on the wall of the hotel.

One picture frame on the wall of the Grand Oriental Hotel. The image shows a framed pencil sketch of three women in traditional attire, likely from a historical or cultural setting. They are gathered outdoors, with one seated on the ground and the others standing, possibly in conversation. The scene includes architectural elements like columns and a balustrade.

Chapter 4: Day 2, From Colombo to Kandy Via Train

Next on day 2 I had my train towards Kandy around 6 AM morning from Colombo Fort railway station.

You can see the colombo fort station in the above picture. At the Colombo fort station there is plenty of space to sit , and the station is not very crowded . You can take your ticket from the ticket counter and wait till your train comes . Make sure to have a conversation with the local official at the train station if you don't understand station number and journey time etc.

You can see one of the trains at Colombo fort railway station. Station officers were helpful to help me find my train platform number. At Colombo Fort Station, trains adorned in vibrant red and yellow hues proudly display their numbers. Impeccably maintained, each carriage gleams with cleanliness. Passengers embark upon these colorful trains, experiencing not only efficient transportation but also a journey marked by comfort and a commitment to hygiene.

Colombo fort railway station early morning in the above picture. You can see a large display board for advertisements having PayHere advertisements. PayHere is an online payment gateway based in Colombo, Sri Lanka, offering secure payment solutions for businesses. It facilitates convenient transactions for e-commerce platforms, allowing customers to pay seamlessly through various payment methods.

I already had a booking via the website and carried a valid print out of the same ticket taken from the station officer.

You can see there is a note on how to open the door and this compartment is fully AC luxury compartment. Washrooms are also very clean and you will also get guidance from train officials if you ask them any queries related to your travel journey.

This is the compartment where my seat was allocated . There are many classes when you book the tickets online. I booked the AC Saloon as I wanted to sleep nicely during the journey breaks.

Thankfully there was no rush and crowd on the railway station and in the compartment too. I was able to sleep nicely on the train till I reached kandy.

Some capture of the journey of Kandy .

The above photograph I took while I was traveling and it was my very first experience for me to travel by Srilankan train. I will suggest you book your train tickets first using the website as later you may find difficulty once you are on your journey date.

The Class S14 trains in Sri Lanka are a modern addition to the country's railway network. These trains, part of the Sri Lanka Railways fleet, offer comfortable and efficient transportation for passengers, featuring air-conditioned carriages and modern amenities to enhance the travel experience.

Kandy railway station in above picture. I really liked the texture and board used for writing the name of the train station.

Some information about the tooth relic brought to Sri Lanka .

When I came out of the train station I decided to walk towards Kandy city center and visit places whichever came across.

I started walking towards the given direction.

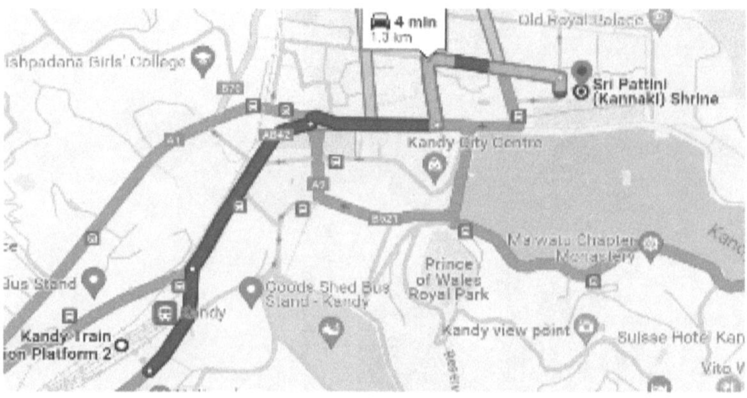

Walking towards **Sri Pattini(Kannaki) Shrine**. The above map will help you find how you can take the route you can use your phone while traveling.

I took these flowers from one of the vendors present outside the shrine. Many people buy these flower sets before entering the temple. I feel this is the ritual here.

Offering flowers holds profound significance in many religious and spiritual traditions, including devotion to various deities. In Hinduism, Buddhism, and other faiths, flowers symbolize purity, beauty, and impermanence. Presenting them to a deity is an act of reverence, expressing devotion, gratitude, and humility towards the divine.

The above image shows a serene Gautam Buddha sitting gracefully, draped in white, embodying tranquility and enlightenment, with an aura of peaceful wisdom surrounding him.

When I came out of the Shrine I started walking on the road randomly , and I was able to capture this picture of a very old building present nearby.

You can find this building once you come out of the temple . I liked the architecture of this building while towards the coffee break.

I decided to take a caffeine break , after coming out of the Shrine for some time.

I saw one cafe in front of **St . Paul's Church.** St. Paul's Church in Kandy is a historic Anglican church, renowned for its colonial architecture and serene atmosphere amidst lush surroundings.

After some time I started walking towards **Kandy Lake .**

You can find this road when you start walking towards the Kandy lake. The road is not that crowded and is very clean and well maintained. The buildings and apartment architecture are also very nice.

This is the photo I have taken at Kandy lake. The water was very clean and the environment was also good. As dusk descends over Kandy

Lake, the scenery transforms into a picturesque spectacle. The tranquil waters mirror the vibrant hues of the setting sun, while the lush surroundings are bathed in golden light, creating a mesmerizing ambiance of serenity and natural beauty.

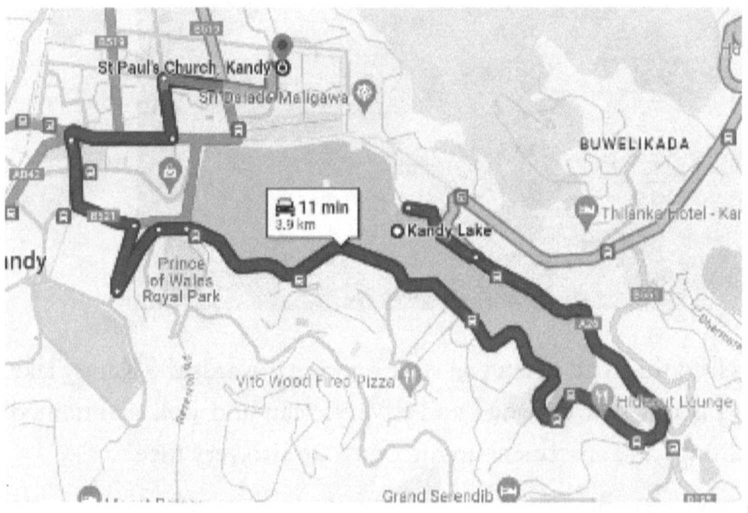

While walking on the road towards Kandy lake I have been to **Kandy city center** too and various other shops nearby .

Dilmah tea is very famous in SriLanka. Dilmah's specialty is single-origin Ceylon tea, handpicked fresh and packed at the source for pure taste. They focus on traditional methods for a richer, more varied flavor compared to mass-produced varieties.

While traveling in Sri Lanka I found this tea is of the best quality , you can always take **BOP** tea anywhere in good cafes in Sri Lanka.

While walking towards Kandy city center I found this beautiful cafe called Cafe Walk.

Above are the menu items and prices are mentioned in LKR. All the menu items are good. I had some snacks and coffee here. I liked the way they have mentioned all types of coffees in a single board which they are serving. There are other items as well which they serve , you can get quality food and coffee here. After the cafe walk , I went straight inside the mall where this cafe is located.

Above picture is from the mall. Some kids are playing in this mall. To my surprise, a music event was also going on in the mall. This mall is located at the central place of Kandy and is really crowded at evening time . Families come along with their kids to enjoy the mall and surroundings.

If you want to use the Sri Lanka post , this office exists in this mall.

The Sri Lanka Post Office in Kandy City Center serves as a bustling
hub of communication and postal services. Nestled within the heart of

the city, it offers a range of mailing and courier solutions, enveloped in a blend of traditional architecture and modern convenience, catering to locals and tourists alike.

Sri Lanka post office inside Kandy city center. But this office was closed when I visited this place. I wanted to see some srilankan stamps to have them in my collection.

In the above picture you can see Kandy City Center. Kandy City Center is a vibrant shopping and entertainment complex in the heart of Kandy, Sri Lanka. Boasting a diverse array of retail outlets, dining options, and entertainment facilities, it attracts visitors seeking shopping, dining, leisure, and cultural experiences in one convenient location.

In the above image you can see the ceylon tea cabin , where you can taste authentic Srilankan tea. The Ceylon Tea Cabin in Kandy is a charming retreat nestled amidst verdant tea gardens. It exudes a cozy ambiance, offering exquisite Ceylon tea varieties and delectable treats, inviting visitors to savor the essence of Sri Lanka's tea culture amid tranquil surroundings.

As I started walking towards the Kandy train station for the Hatton train , I took the tea in the above shop.

You can find this ceylon tea cabin at the given location .

This was a great experience taking tea before starting my next journey towards Hatton.

I started walking towards the Kandy train station as I wanted to travel towards Hatton. This train was around 5 PM in the evening.

You can take some snacks at this outlet at Kandy railway station .

I had a look towards the electricity meters installed , I found them very nice as they are very old but they were still maintained and in working condition. Old electricity meters in Sri Lanka are rugged, mechanical devices with spinning dials, measuring power consumption. They evoke nostalgia for simpler times amidst modern technology.

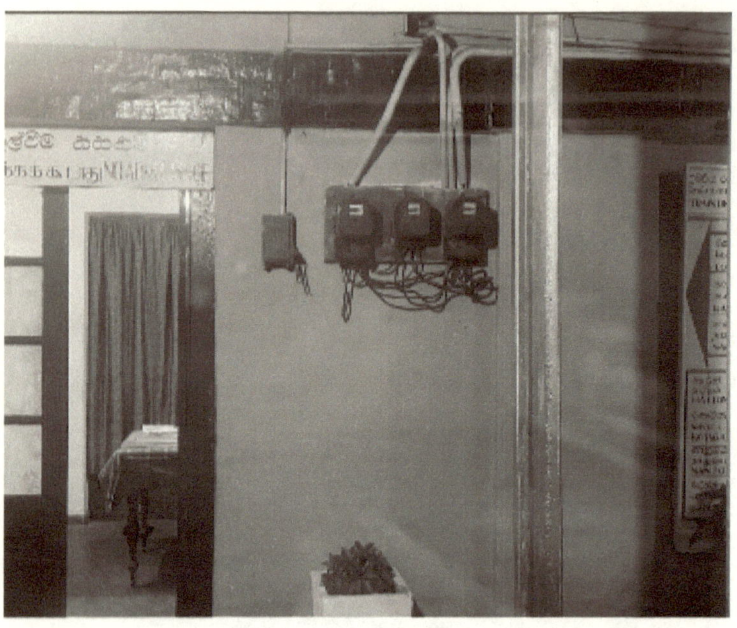

My ticket towards Hatton was booked , so I took the train.

After reaching Hatton at night around 8:30 PM. I started my journey towards my guest house Hugging clouds at Hatton.

The roads were very narrow towards the guest house at night.

I had a look at the start point of Adam's peak near my guest house .

Hugging Clouds has a great cafe in the guest house. I saw the coffee menu .I liked the espresso which I took here .

This espresso was served in a very nice cup of Nescafe . I discussed my plans with the owner of the guest house early in the morning. I told him I wanted to visit Nuwara Eliya first , New Zealand farms and nearby areas. There was cab and taxi service available with the guest house . I started early in the morning around 9 AM from the guest house towards New Zealand farm and Sita Amman temple.

Chapter 5: Day 3 in Nuwara Eliya

I have started taking a few pictures on my journey towards Nuwara Eliya.

You can see many tea farms on your route and have amazing views of various reservoirs and tea plantations where you can take great pictures and videos. But you must start your journey early in the morning.

Vibrant tea plantation: Rolling hills adorned with lush green tea bushes, under a clear sky, showcasing the natural beauty of cultivation.

Some reservoirs along the journey. You will get a very nice view via this journey from Hatton .

Driver stopped our car near very nice and beautiful church called as **Christ Church Warleigh, Dickoya**

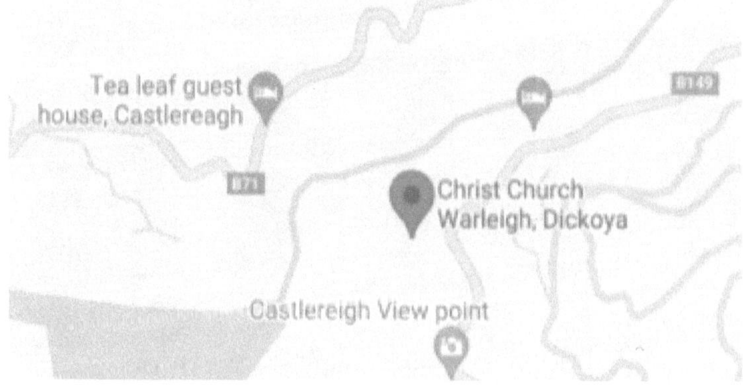

The above location you can use while traveling to the church.

The above image you can observe before entering into the church.

Christ Church Warleigh, Dickoya, is a charming Anglican church nestled amidst the lush greenery of Sri Lanka's hill country. Built in the late 19th century, its quaint architecture and serene surroundings offer a tranquil retreat for worshipers and visitors seeking solace and spiritual reflection amidst natural beauty.

The church serves as a significant religious and cultural landmark, hosting regular services and community events. Its picturesque setting amidst tea plantations adds to its allure, attracting tourists and pilgrims alike.

I had a discussion with church caretakers as well , the photography inside of the church was not allowed but it is really beautiful inside the church too. The caretaker explained the various events that happen in the church and various activities his family has been managing for many years.

There are many old graves near the church from the 1800 and 1900 era. Can't post images here due to privacy concerns. I asked the caretaker about people from the family coming here to have remembrance about the people buried here ? To that he replied , yes people come after finding them via references .

This church is a must visit for peace and to see great architecture. As I was discussing with the caretaker inside the church there are very old items like musical instruments kept inside the church and a few old bibles. You must visit the church from inside , also they preserve the register for many years for visitors , make your entry inside the register.

I told my cab driver to stop at some good point to have breakfast and tea.

We found this hotel Maharaja Grand and decided to have breakfast and tea.

Inside the hotel there is a tea showcase as well where you can select if you want any specific tea of your choice.

You can take some tea bags if you want . But I was very hungry and decided to have BOP tea first and then take some dishes from the menu item.

I ordered Dilmah BOP tea.

This tea was really nice and was of great quality . You must take Dilmah tea during your journey in Sri Lanka.

As I was discussing with the cab driver , I told him to check if we can visit any tea factory during the journey so he said he will try . I replied ok lets see how it goes.

Many tea factories were on the journey but we stopped here for a factory visit.

Craigie Lea Estate . This was a great factory visit. Can't post images here due to restrictions as this was my personal visit . Tea factories play a pivotal role in the global tea industry, processing freshly harvested tea leaves into various grades and types of tea. They ensure quality control, preserve flavors, and meet market demands. Beyond economic significance, they are cultural icons, shaping livelihoods and landscapes in tea-growing regions worldwide.

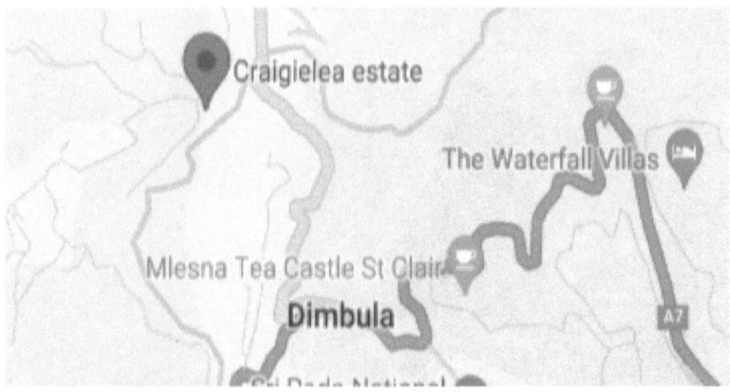

Above map image you can use to find out the tea estate and visit by taking the permission.

I understood the tea processing in detail from officers. I captured a few pictures after my visit to the tea factory.

Vivid green grass stretches beneath majestic mountains, creating a serene landscape of natural beauty and tranquility, inviting awe and reverence.

We again stopped for the tea and I took premium BOPF black tea. Below given image shows the menu items for various type of tea.

We were moving towards the New Zealand Farm at Nuwara Eliya. I started taking more pictures of the great nature out of my window.

This is the **Sita Amman Temple** . entrance gate . The Sita Amman Temple, located in Nuwara Eliya, Sri Lanka, is a sacred Hindu site dedicated to Sita, wife of Lord Rama. Surrounded by lush greenery, it features a serene atmosphere and a shrine honoring Sita's devotion. Pilgrims visit to seek blessings and immerse themselves in spiritual tranquility.

You can use the above map location to visit this temple.

Above image shows the entrance gate for the temple.

Sita Amman Temple's entrance: Ornate gates adorned with intricate carvings.

Sita Amman Temple's renowned feature is the Hanuman footprint, a revered symbol of devotion, myth, and spirituality, nestled within the tranquil surroundings of Nuwara Eliya.

As we were traveling I was discussing purchasing the premium tea with Dilip (my cab driver) . He told me that he will stop at the correct shop to purchase great tea. We got to this great tea shop during the journey , it is the official tea sales center of Sri Lanka tea board.

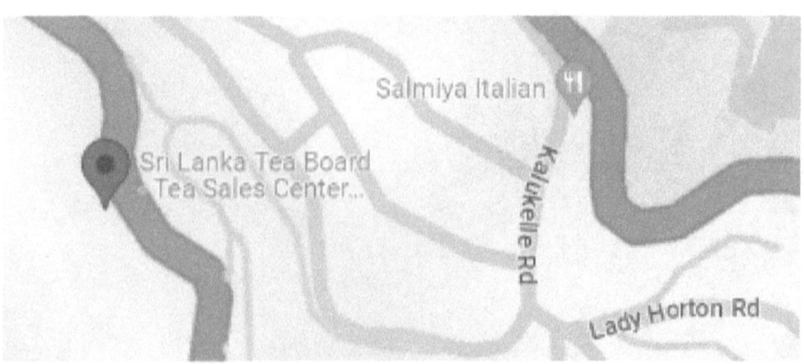

As I entered the shop I was amazed to see many varieties and flavors of the tea . I told the salesman to give some 2-3 samples to taste and then I will select from it. They agreed and we had 3 different varieties of tea including BOPF , earl gray and lemon.

I personally liked BOPF and I took a few other tea items as a gift once I returned back to India.

They have a good sitting area where you can sit and enjoy your tea with friends or in solitude. Dilip and I enjoyed this tea tasting session .

As I already said I wanted to visit the New Zealand farm at Nuwara Eliya after this tea session we immediately started our journey towards the **New Zealand farm.**

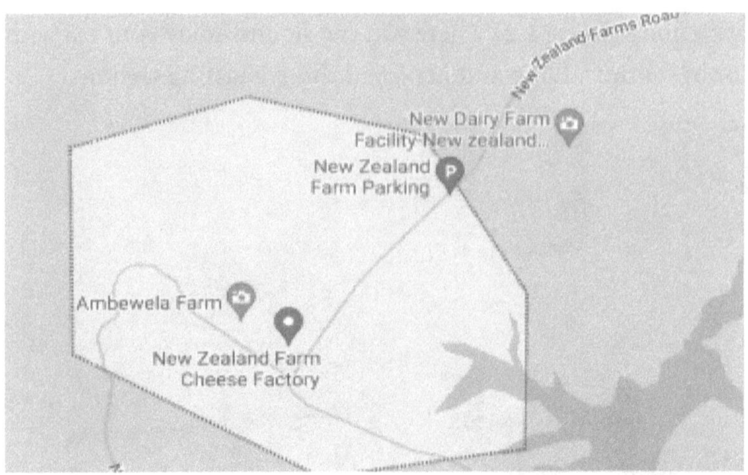

One of the roads towards this farm was closed then we took another route towards the farm. I already had a discussion with my friend about this farm. He told me there are many rabbits here on the farm and a very good description I have heard about this farm from him .

As we reached this farm we took the tickets and went inside the farm immediately as I wanted to visit this farm before closing time , we were already late .

In the above images you can find the board and decide whether you are at the correct location or not.

You can see in the above image that the tank is getting filled by fresh milk , I think it is getting ready for supply.

In the above image you can see basic farm facilities .

This farm is very big and has good facilities and features for getting good quality milk.

The climate here is chilly, so don't forget to pack warm sweaters to stay cozy amidst the crisp, cold air.

In the picture, a neat row of trees stands tall, each one meticulously cared for with evident dedication. Their lush foliage and healthy appearance reflect the meticulous attention paid to their growth, showcasing a harmonious blend of nature and human stewardship in nurturing these green guardians of the earth.

There are many other animals as well in the farm. I started taking pictures as I went inside the farm for more exploration.

The following sign board is visible inside the farm that will guide you for various places.

You have to find such sign boards to visit each and every corner of the Ambewela farm here. Look at the sign boards everywhere and don't miss any of the places inside the farm.

This is some other sign board guiding towards the restaurant of the New Zealand farm.

One should always visit the restaurant and have coffee with fresh milk.

Above images shows the way to farm fresh cafe.

I liked the restaurant a lot and tasted the great coffee I had here. There are other food items too that you can taste , those are very fresh and tasty.

They serve coffee this way in a big mug and you can enjoy this in the restaurant. Then I visited the Rabbit department too for which I came here.

New Arrival From France
F1 Gen Male Rabbits Are
Now Available
For Sale – Rs.2,000/-
(For Breeding)
PS HYLA OPTIMA (M60)
Rabbits a
Po

After visiting many other departments I decided to move back to my guest house at Hugging clouds as we were getting late.

Cleanliness at this farm is amazing .Washroom facilities are available here for your convenience.

It was raining heavily as I started moving towards the car with Dilip (cab driver) .

This dog was not allowing us to go back . So I took his picture as a remembrance.

I took the final pictures of the New Zealand farm and said bye to Nuwara Eliya.

This is a New Zealand farm during the evening time. We started moving towards the **Hugging clouds guest house** from **New Zealand Farm.**I slept for some time in the car as Dilip was driving the car.

We observed some ritual for Adam's peak visit as we were traveling towards the guest house. You can see in the above picture that man is carrying lights , Dilip said it's some ritual.

We spotted this bird in the car light during the journey and I took the picture.

I was able to zoom to this level only. This bird was not moving even if
our car was very near but after my camera movement it went in the next
5 minutes . I wanted to capture many movements but was not able to
do so.

Finally we reached the guest house and I slept immediately , before this I said thanks to Dilip for this great journey.

Chapter 6: Day 4 in Adam's Peak

After my journey on the last day , I decided to cover a few other travel points on Day 4 on my journey. I was staying at **Hugging Clouds Guest house** only for this day as well.

This guest house is very much near to Adams Peak but I was not sure whether to cover this or not. Owner told me you can cover this Peak very easily. This entire day was unplanned for me.

When I woke up I saw beautiful scenery in front of my room.

My room was perfectly located in front of the natural garden with a very nice view.

I took some pictures of the guest house as well. Today I wanted to rest and relax a bit . I started taking pictures of the guest house and nearby areas of this guest house.

This is the guest house cafe and entrance for the guest house. It's very clean and beautiful.

When I stepped out of the guest house for a walk I saw a Toyota Carina car . I really liked the build of this car , I took a few pictures of it.

The Toyota Carina offers a blend of reliability, comfort, and practicality with features like efficient engines, spacious interiors, advanced safety systems, and intuitive technology.

As time passed I decided to walk towards Adams Peak and complete today's journey.

I started walking towards Adams Peak .

Sri Pada, also known as Adam's Peak, is a sacred mountain in Sri Lanka revered by multiple religions. Its ascent embodies devotion, unity, and reverence amidst breathtaking natural beauty.

As I was walking towards Adams Peak I started capturing many photos for various places coming in front of me.

As you walk towards Adams Peak you can see many boards for information about this place.

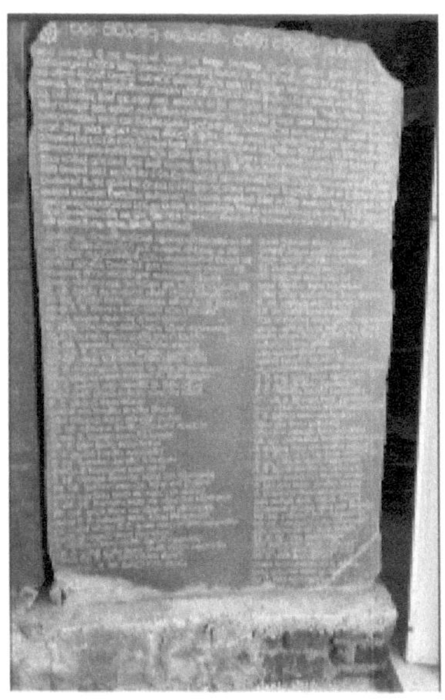

I found this script written on stone while walking. In the image, scriptures carved on stone endure as timeless guardians of wisdom and faith. Immune to time's passage, these inscriptions transcend generations, preserving teachings, laws, and stories. They serve as tangible links to our cultural and spiritual heritage, guiding and inspiring seekers on their journey through the annals of human history.

I decided to take a tea at some shop.

The shopkeeper was very nice and supportive . I liked the tea which he gave me.

It energized me for my remaining journey towards the Peak.

He showed me a TV stand for selling which he has made on his own. I told him to stand near this stand so that I could capture the picture of him.

After taking his picture and having the tea I restarted my journey towards the Peak. I was not in a hurry to complete the Peak in minimum time as I have completely dedicated this entire day for this Peak only. I have decided to slowly meet more people, understand the culture and explore this beautiful place.

I took many pictures on this journey.

Infrastructure and roads are very nice towards the Peak. The image captures the impeccable infrastructure surrounding Adams Peak, exemplified by a gracefully constructed bridge. The roads winding through the landscape reflect thoughtful planning and engineering, enhancing accessibility to this revered pilgrimage site. Such meticulous attention to detail underscores a harmonious blend of modernity and reverence for nature's splendor.

There are many washrooms available as you walk towards the Peak , you can take enough breaks , take rest and then start again. There is no rush .

You can find loudspeakers on the trees which play religious songs and are used for announcements too. The pathway to Adams Peak resonates with the soul-stirring melodies of religious hymns emanating from strategically placed loudspeakers. These musical guides not only uplift spirits but also offer direction and solace to pilgrims on their spiritual journey. Amidst nature's grandeur, the songs serve as harmonious companions, echoing devotion along the sacred trail.

While walking I came across this Ayurvedic shop. They were selling some Ayurvedic drinks , you can taste the drink here for free , have some water and purchase the items from them if you wish . This is a good point to stop for some time and continue towards your journey.

Just have a look at this beautiful scenery while I was climbing towards the Adams peak. Temperature was very cool and the environment was super thrilling.

As evening descends upon Adams Peak, the summit unveils a breathtaking panorama of majestic mountains, meandering rivers, and lush natural beauty. The soft hues of twilight enhance the scene, casting a spellbinding aura over the landscape. It's a mesmerizing spectacle that beckons awe and reverence amidst nature's grandeur.

You can see the cleanliness and how the advertisement for cleanliness is done .

Finally I came towards the last tea shop of Adams peak and took the picture near this point.

I also took the tea here to enjoy the environment and clean air. For some time I took rest here for about 5 minutes after having my tea.

Took this photograph as evidence that I went to Adams Peak at the last tea shop.

Photography was not allowed after this point , but the temple , cleanliness and my experience here was really nice , people are very nice and supportive . I was here around 4:30 PM , and attended the evening prayer as well.

Evening view from top of Adam's peak looks like this.

After the temple visit and prayers , I spent more time here and decided on my journey back to the guest house to have coffee and dinner.

I started my journey using stairs going down .

You can find many shops for keychains, some photographs etc. You can take them for you or your friends. I took some keychains.

I was able to find an Electrical management unit as well.

You can find a sleeping Buddha once you come down.

In the image, the Sleeping Buddha reclines in serene repose, embodying tranquility and eternal peace. His graceful posture, with one hand supporting his head and the other resting gently by his side, exudes a sense of profound serenity and spiritual enlightenment, inviting contemplation and reverence.

There is Lord Ganesh temple as well beside sleeping buddha temple.

After so much struggle for the day , I wanted to go back to my guest house for a great espresso and relax.

I had Espresso at my guest house. After taking the espresso and some rest , I decided to have dinner outside of the guest house. So I started walking on the road to find a good restaurant.

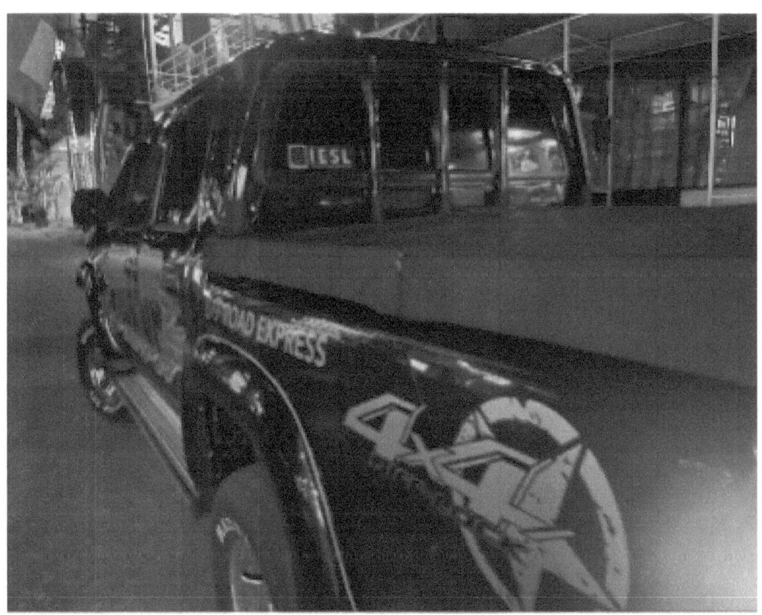

I found this beautiful car while I was walking to find a good restaurant. Finally I found a good restaurant.

And then I had my dinner here on this long table . After the dinner I went to the guest house and slept nicely.

Chapter 7: Day 5 in Pinnawala

Today is December 29th.

This day and my plan was not fully decided , I wanted to visit Galle too as I have read many great things about this place and wanted to visit Hikkaduwa beach and surroundings. I have my train ticket from Colombo to Galle but that was on 31st december and today it is 29th december , So I was not knowing what to do . I discussed it with the owner of the guest house , after that I agreed to visit Pinnawala with his cab driver as he also had some guests to pick from Colombo Airport so the cab driver could drop me near Pinnawala. I agreed to this plan and decided to visit Pinnawala zoo.

Till the cab came I decided to explore the cafe in the guest house.

This is the cafe and shopping setup they have inside the guest house so you do need to go out for snacks and regular needs. I liked this concept and appreciated the owner for this.

Today I had cappuccino and it was fantastic.

I took some photos with the guest house architecture.

Took one photo with the owner of this guest house .

This map is present in the guest house which can help you decide where you can go , if you are a traveler like me who decides the places on the go and not always preplanned.

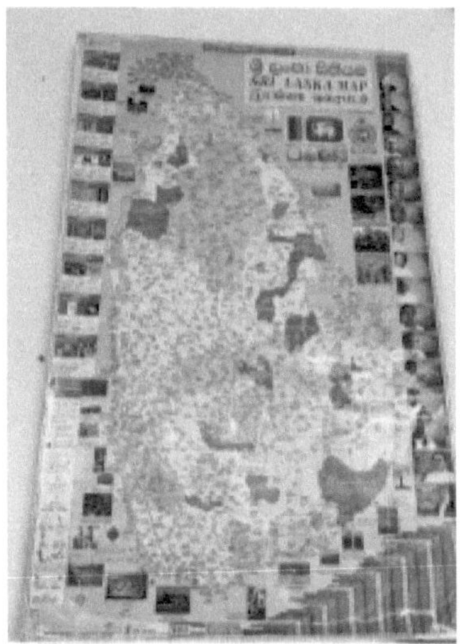

The above given map is present at Hugging clouds guest house . You can take reference from this map. Dilip (Cab driver) and I started my journey towards Pinnawala zoo after discussion with the guest house owner.

During the journey I felt like visiting various grocery shops to purchase cold coffee or some biscuits during the journey . Dilip was not feeling well , so we stopped by there for sometime.

I entered one of the supermarkets to purchase some biscuits and cold drinks. The picture depicts a bustling scene at a vibrant market, with an array of noodles and cold drinks enticing passersby. Amidst the colorful displays, the supermarket stands out for its exceptional staff service, radiating warmth and efficiency. It's a haven for shoppers, offering both culinary delights and top-notch customer care.

There are so many varieties available at this shop .

This outlet I guess is **Lanka Santhosa** .

As we were going towards Pinnawala we stopped nearby for lunch . Dilip (Cab driver) suggested to me one good hotel where we decided to have food.

We stopped near the **Village Restaurant**. It's very near to **Gampola**.

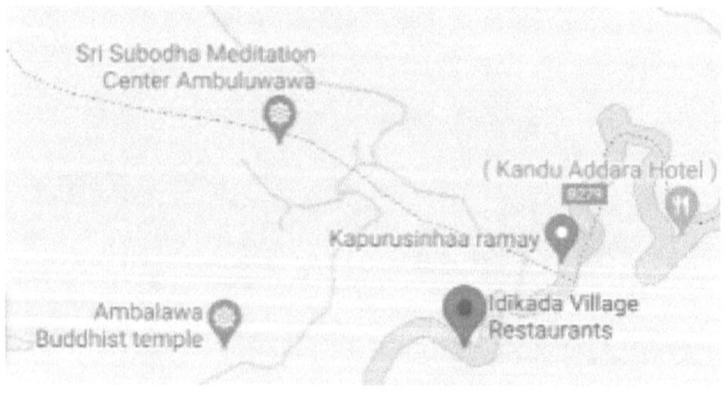

You can take reference of the above map for finding out the restaurant .

Captured in the image is a delightful encounter with the owner of a charming eatery, where personalized service meets culinary excellence. With attentive care, the owner crafts delectable dishes tailored to individual tastes and preferences, creating a memorable dining experience filled with warmth, hospitality, and gastronomic delight.

We got one photo with him then. We had a discussion on various topics during lunch time.

This is how food is served in this restaurant . You will get very nice and fresh authentic Srilankan food.

I don't remember the name of this Roti now but if you are having a look at it now then you should and must order this .

After this great lunch we started driving towards my **Suwani Pinnawala guest house** which I have already checked on google maps. I have already booked this in advance . We reached here around 5 PM , Dilip took some rest here and went for his Colombo pickup . I thanked him for all his help. He was very helpful during my stay near Adams peak , tour near Eliya Nuwara and finally journey towards Pinnawala.

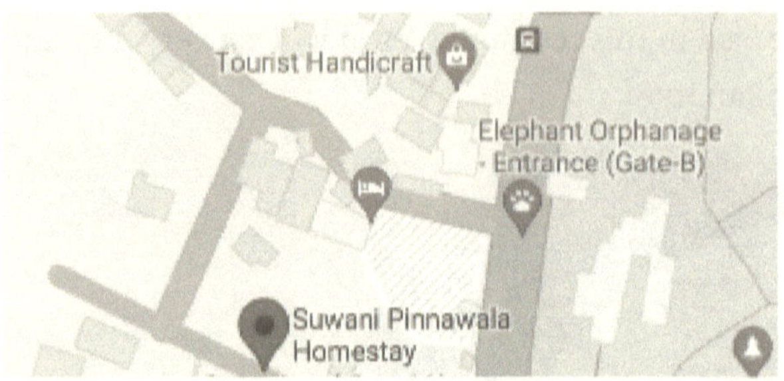

Use the given map for finding out the Suwani Pinnawala homestay.

I took some rest today in the guest house . Owner asked me what kind of breakfast I would like to have the next day. I asked her to prepare any local dish which she wanted to prepare and prepare coffee as well.

I slept early today because I wanted to visit Pinnawala elephant zoo and Orphanage the next day. I asked her all the procedures about the visit to these places and she was very helpful and guided me very well.

Chapter 8: Day 6 in Pinnawala

Today is December 30th.

I have already done my train booking towards Colombo fort for 31st december , from Colombo I will be traveling to Galle on the same day.

I woke up early this day around 6:30 AM . To my surprise breakfast was ready for me around 7 AM .

I don't recall the name of this dish but it was really tasty and delicious too. You have to use the given curry with these food items and eat. I was able to find coffee as well for me made using french press.

After drinking the coffee I felt relaxed and fresh and I was ready to explore Pinnawala for the entire day.

Pinnawala zoo is very near to this guest house. If you are from the SAARC country list you can get the ticket discount at the orphanage and zoo. Just carry the required documents. I took the ticket and started exploring the Orphanage.

I started walking inside the orphanage.

I got to know the elephant's bathing time was there and started walking towards the river .

An elephant shop sells eco-friendly products made from elephant dung, creatively transforming waste into paper, crafts, and souvenirs, promoting sustainability and conservation.

There are many elephant dung products available if you wish to buy.

This is the place elephant bathing will be done. You can watch this from a nearby location of your choice as guided by officials.

Officials started bringing elephants for bathing. I was there in the nearby restaurant to enjoy coffee and this river bathing of elephants.

In the above image you can see a person is using the pipe to bathe elephants.

A man sprays water on elephants with a pipe, the gentle stream cascading over their backs, creating a refreshing and intimate bathing experience.

I was enjoying the coffee as well in the restaurant and watching this bathing. You can take your selfies too and you will surely take the same.

I saw buskers with snakes who are performing here. Captured in the image is a mesmerizing sight: a husker and a snake poised together on the roadside, ready to captivate passersby with their enthralling performance. Amidst the hustle and bustle of the street, this unlikely duo commands attention, showcasing a unique blend of skill, courage, and harmony between man and serpent.

I was very impressed with these face masks. I wanted to buy one but didn't buy one because of the limitation of traveling bags.

I started walking towards the Orphanage for more information and other points to visit. I saw this coconuts and decided to have coconut water here.

The above coconuts were very tasty and the water was really sweet. This person sits near the elephant orphanage and sells it.

You can find this board near the orphanage .

Also there is a guide .

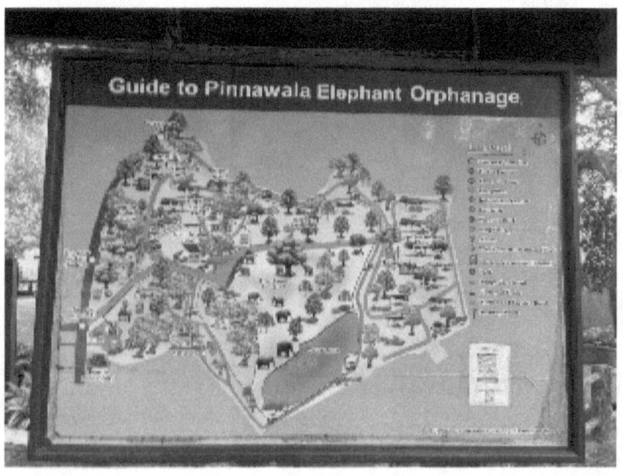

You can use this guide to visit all the spots in the orphanage.

I liked this architecture. They have created nice art using a collection of elephants.

I found this beautiful cat in the elephant orphanage.

Everyone was running to see the elephants and this cat was actually feeling lonely , so I captured some photos of this cat. Cat in an elephant orphanage isn't quite interesting ?

Next I moved to another spot where many people were feeding fruits to elephants.

You can get fruits inside the orphanage and officials will help you understand the process.

You can get more information about elephants in the orphanage just have a look at boards everywhere.

This park is also inside an elephant orphanage. Nestled in the heart of Pinnawala, PBG Kalugalla Park is a verdant oasis of tranquility. Amidst the bustling town, this serene sanctuary offers respite with its lush greenery, scenic pathways, and serene atmosphere.

By observing an elephant's teeth, one can estimate its age as each set of teeth emerges at different stages of life, providing clues to its approximate age.

These are the tools used by Mahouts displayed here. A mahout is an elephant handler or keeper, typically found in regions where elephants are domesticated, responsible for caring for and guiding these majestic animals.

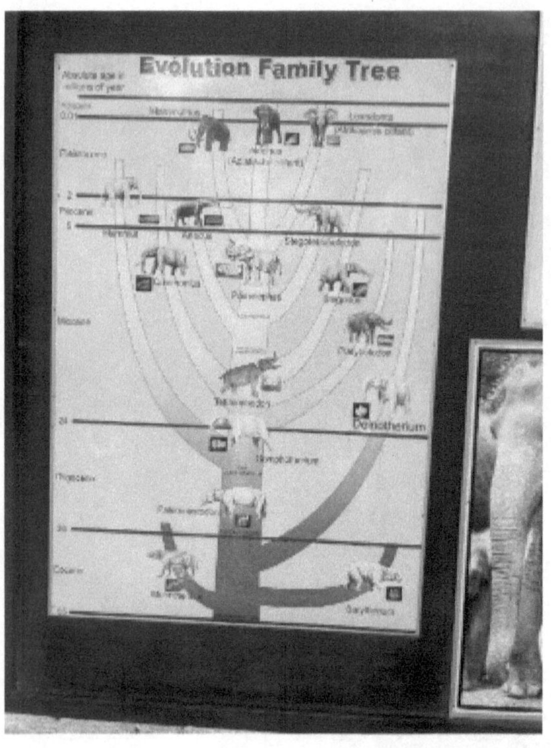

You can find about the evolution of family trees for elephants as well.

You can find more information about Sumana the tusker .

I found this elephant playing with water . An elephant gleefully dabbles in a small pond, its trunk dipping into the water, creating ripples of delight amidst serene surroundings.

I completed the journey to the orphanage and then I started walking towards the Pinnawala zoo.

This is the entrance of the Pinnawala zoo. The entrance to Pinnawala Zoo welcomes visitors with grand gates adorned with intricate carvings, set amidst lush greenery and vibrant flora.

Use the above given map location to reach the correct location of Pinnawala zoo. You can find the below given map inside the zoo.

The above map will help you to visit most of the places available in the zoo.

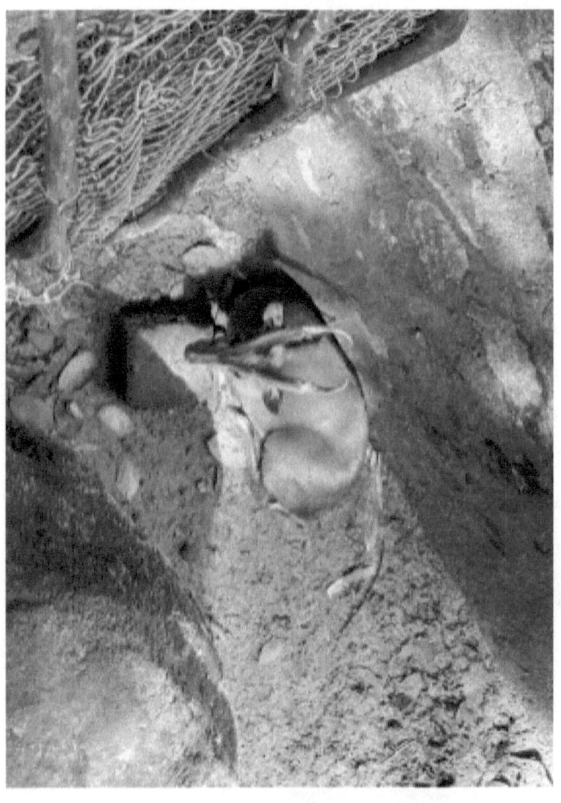

The moose, also known as the moose deer, is a large herbivorous mammal characterized by its imposing size, distinctive antlers, and formidable presence in northern ecosystems.

There are numbers in front of the sites so you easily map and locate .

The emu, native to Australia, is a flightless bird characterized by its tall stature, long neck, powerful legs, and distinctive feathers.I really liked Emu and his walking style.

Roads are very clean inside the zoo. Within the zoo, pristine roads wind through well-maintained landscapes, showcasing impeccable cleanliness and organization. Lined with lush greenery and thoughtfully designed enclosures, these paths offer visitors a seamless journey through the animal habitats. The commitment to cleanliness enhances the overall experience, ensuring a pleasant and hygienic environment for all.

The zoo was not crowded during this time , so I was able to spend more time peacefully inside the zoo and take photographs peacefully. You can also find many Aquatic birds here.

Aquatic birds, adapted for life in water, include ducks, swans, and herons. They possess waterproof feathers, webbed feet, and long necks for foraging underwater.

I found a crocodile enclosure too. The crocodile enclosure in the park features a secure habitat with clear viewing areas, allowing visitors to observe these ancient reptiles in their natural habitat. There is so much information written about crocodiles on the walls here.

I really liked this bird sitting alone inside the water on top of wood. I took many photographs of him.

If you come along with your family or friends in a group you can enjoy this place and spend some time near this location and capture many photographs here.

I was coming near the Leopard and Bear enclosure. The leopard enclosure in the park offers a spacious and naturalistic habitat for these majestic big cats, with elevated platforms and dense foliage providing ample opportunities for observation. Nearby, the bear enclosure simulates a forest environment, complete with rocky outcrops and lush vegetation, ensuring a comfortable and stimulating environment for the bears.

This leopard was sitting quietly and I got the chance to click a photo of him.

If you are thirsty you can drink water from such an amazing place. You can find a leopard cave nearby . It has all the information related to leopards.

Seating space inside a leopard enclosure cave. This is a great experience . After visiting this cave I came out and started looking for other places to visit.

I found these beautiful gardens and flower trees. In the park, vibrant red flowers bloom in abundance, their delicate petals unfurling like flames against the lush green backdrop. Their beauty captivates passersby, attracting bees and butterflies with their sweet nectar. Amidst the tranquility of the park, these crimson blooms add a touch of elegance and charm.

I came out of this cave too.

There is this beautiful place where you can click photos and sit for sometime.

This was there for couples I guess . I saw many couples enjoying taking photographs here. In the park, a romantic display unfolds with heart-shaped flower decorations adorning pathways and benches, creating a whimsical atmosphere for couples. Vibrant blooms cascade in crimson hues, evoking love and passion.

There is a National zoo academy as well but entry was restricted here.

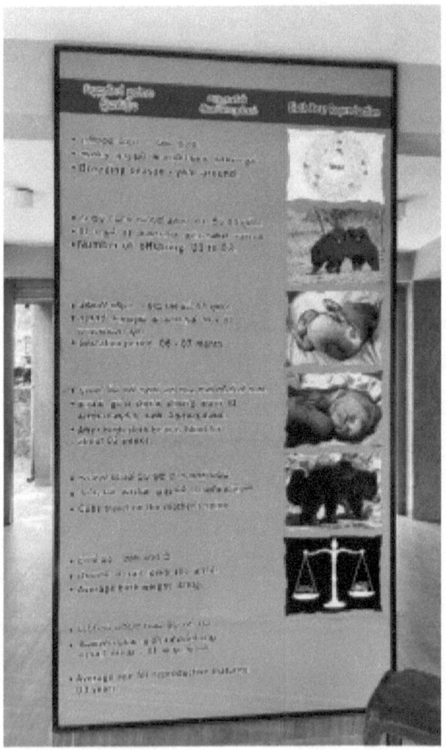

There is a bear enclosure as well , you can spot many bears and more information about bears in this enclosure.

There is a butterfly park too. You will get more information about it while you walk towards it. Make sure you are holding a photo of the park so that you can easily locate each and every part of the zoo.

The Blue and Gold Macaw, is a strikingly beautiful parrot native to South America.Its vibrant plumage features a deep blue color on its upperparts and a bright yellow on its underparts, with touches of green on the wings.

Finally , my entire journey was completed for this zoo. When you come out of the zoo you can find this place in front of the exit gate of the zoo.

Either you can visit or have snacks nearby

I had some evening snacks here.

When I saw this I immediately decided to have this and taste.

Captured in the image is a delectable plate of tender jackfruit cutlet. The jackfruit's mild sweetness melds with aromatic spices, tantalizing the taste buds with a burst of flavors and textures, offering a delightful culinary experience for any palate.

I was very hungry after the elephant orphanage visit and zoo visit. Thankfully this place was exactly opposite the Pinnawala zoo exit gate.

After this I came back to my guest house.

This guest house Suwani Pinnawala is very nice and clean . After some rest I came back on the road of Pinnawala elephant orphanage and started searching for some good coffee or cafe.

I found this great cafe **Paradise of food.**

Use the above given location to reach this cafe. You can get this riverview from this cafe.

The café offers a picturesque vista of the tranquil river meandering through lush greenery, creating a serene backdrop for sipping coffee. From the comfort of rustic chairs, patrons can immerse themselves in nature's splendor, savoring the aroma of freshly brewed coffee amidst the soothing symphony of flowing water and chirping birds.You can enjoy this view around 5 PM till 7 PM with your coffee and sandwich.

These benches are really helpful here as to spend your time with friends or in solitude .

Do you think this isn't a great time to have coffee facing the calm river and in solitude ? Definitely yes. When I came out of the cafe there was a festival going on in Pinnawala Road.

The night sky comes alive with vibrant colors as a lively festival unfolds on the road. Families and children gather amid the bustling atmosphere, enjoying an array of food stalls and engaging in fun activities. Laughter fills the air, creating a festive ambiance of joy and camaraderie under the starlit sky.

When I talked with local people they said it's there at evening time where you can enjoy many food items and there are various games for kids.

After some time I went back to my homestay as I wanted to move back to Colombo and then back to Galle for my next plan.

I showed my tickets to the guest house owner. They said my current ticket to Colombo won't work as it is some super express which doesn't stop at the nearby railway station. Then somehow I managed to understand the new plan from Rambukkana railway station. I can goto Colombo early in the morning and the train won't be very crowded . I took this suggestion from the guest house owner and then finally went to sleep as early in the morning .I will be going to Rambukkana railway station with the owner who is coming to drop me off . It was a great gesture .

Chapter 9: Day 7 in Rambukkana and Galle

Today is 31st December .

I started moving to **Rambukkana railway station** to catch a train early in the morning. We started around 6:15 AM from Pinnawala.

I started taking the photographs on the way as I was in the tuk-tuk.

I reached the station around 6:30 AM. I said goodbye to the guest house owner. He had a conversation with the ticket counter person in the local language for my Colombo journey then I bought the tickets .

This board you can find here displays the time of trains for Colombo , Kandy and Badulla.

When I boarded the train I found this person singing beautiful songs using his guitar.

My journey till Colombo was great due to this good music and ambience. I reached Colombo around 10 AM.

You can see this wooden bridge at the Colombo station.

After reaching Colombo fort I have decided to visit cafes and roasteries in this city. I immediately took a cab towards **Whight & Co Cafe.** You can find many manual brewing equipment present in this cafe.

The above image shows various equipment available for sale for manual coffee brewing. They also have a roasting machine for coffee.

They have named this brand as Ruby Harvest as you can see in the picture. There are few photographs of various coffee estate maps present in this cafe.

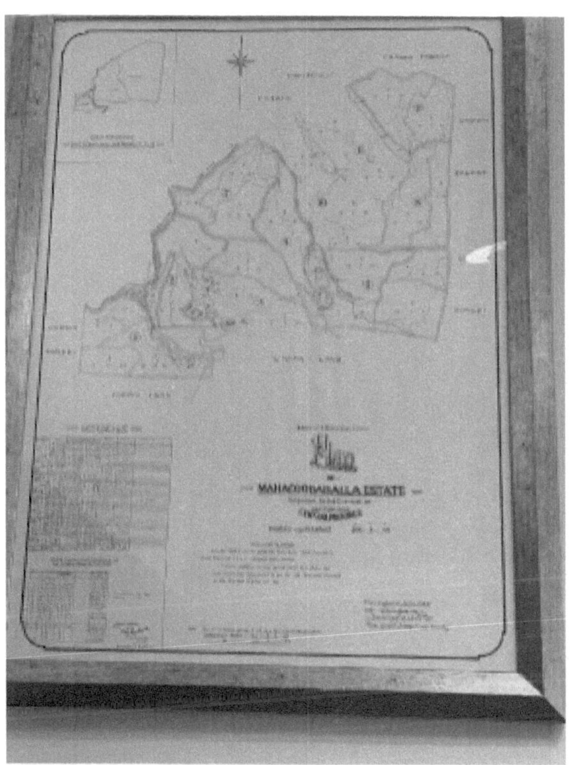

I took an espresso shot here and I really liked it . Due to baggage weight, I didn't buy any coffee beans here. After some time I also visited **Cafe 1959.**

After the cafe visit I immediately went to colombo station to catch the train towards Galle.

I reached Galle station around 5:15 PM. As I reached I found many banners for 31st december celebration across the city. I was already in contact with one of my couch surfing friends. Through my friend I got references with whom I can celebrate today's new year .

After reaching the station I started searching for my guest house which I followed using Google maps. I started walking towards my guest house **COCO Rooms**. Room was very nice and clean.

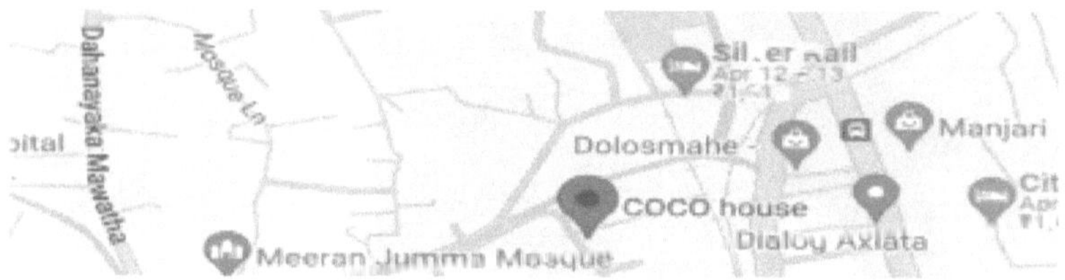

At around 9 PM I reached **Kingfisher Hotel** near Unawatuna Beach.

Use above map location for reaching towards the hotel.

There was this book library in the hotel. I celebrated this new year here in SriLanka with many new friends.

You can see how people were enjoying this new year on the night of 31st december.

After this celebration, I went back to my guest house COCO Rooms.

Chapter 10: Day 8 in Hikkaduwa and Galle

1st January .

This was the new year morning for me in Sri Lanka. I wanted to visit the cafe in Hikkaduwa, namely **Salty Swamis.**

I started my journey by taking the tuk - tuk .

I started taking pictures as I was moving towards Hikkaduwa.

The roads were clean and the ambience was really good. Finally I reached the cafe location.

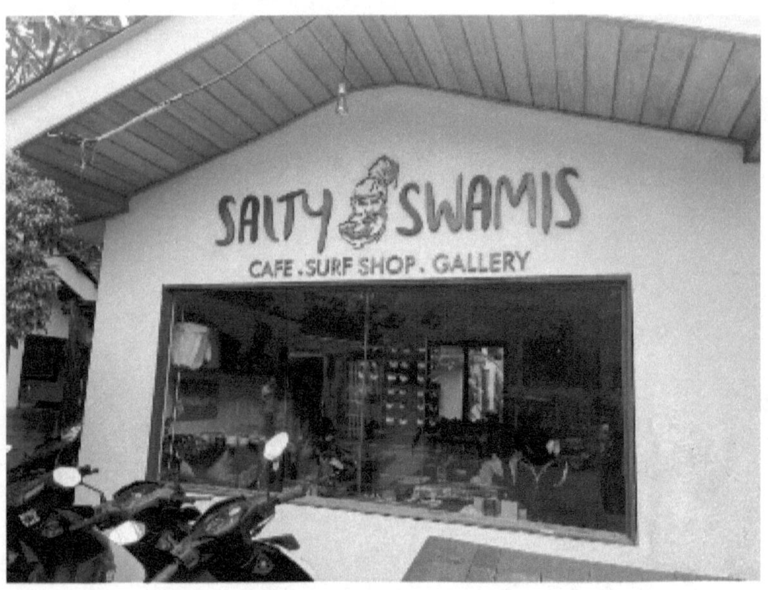

I wanted to taste the coffee here in pour over and latte too. So I ordered them .

The taste of the above coffee was exotic , aromatic . I also had a Latte after this one.

In the image, a steaming cup of latte captures the artistry of a heart-shaped design delicately etched atop the velvety foam. The rich espresso hues swirl gracefully to form the perfect symbol of love and warmth, inviting a moment of sweetness and affection with every sip.The latte art was really nice , and the coffee also was very nice and superb. This cafe also has a beach view. .

Here you can come relax and enjoy your food with coffee. You can see a beautiful beach with your friend in this cafe and enjoy the time .

I was impressed by the wooden art and graphics made inside the cafe. You will get water as shown below.

After this cafe I started walking towards the turtle beach of Hikkaduwa. I found this Sandagiri Supermarket on the road while walking. Sandagiri Supermarket in Hikkaduwa is a bustling hub offering a wide array of goods and services. From fresh produce to household essentials, it caters to the needs of locals and tourists alike. Its vibrant atmosphere and friendly staff make shopping a pleasant experience in this coastal town of Sri Lanka.

You can take a cold drink or grocery if you wish to .

I went near the turtle beach . Turtle Beach in Hikkaduwa is a haven for nature enthusiasts and beach lovers. With its pristine golden sands and crystal-clear waters, it provides a serene backdrop for sunbathing and swimming. Visitors also have the opportunity to witness majestic sea turtles in their natural habitat, adding to the area's allure and charm.

I came back immediately as I wanted to go back to my guest house early and visit other places in Galle too.

I saw many people standing near the bus stop. I also took help from locals to find the bus stop.

I liked the design made inside the bus , you can see it from the above picture. After reaching the galle near the guest house , I went to have lunch around 3 PM at Green corner restaurant near my guest house Coco house. I liked this dish .

I think they call this Egg Kottu. While walking on the roads I found one person in a bungalow having a MORRIS car. I asked him and he told me he has the passion for old cars. I took his photo with the car.

Car looks very nice from the front view. I took pictures of this car.

I had some discussion about his passion for cars for sometime and then went to visit other places in Galle around 4 PM.

I started walking towards **Galle Fort.**

City is nicely managed and it has separate lanes for cycles too.

This is the information map present at the place where you can take help to visit all the places as per the map. The old town of Galle boasts historic charm with its well-preserved fortifications, showcasing colonial architecture and a rich cultural heritage amidst picturesque surroundings.

There was sudden rain when I started walking towards the fort.

You can see the roads in the fort are clean and the architecture is really beautiful .

Canon's are present at the fort. At Galle Fort, ancient cannons stand
sentinel, reminders of bygone eras and strategic defense, adding
historical intrigue to the coastal fortress.The cannons at Galle Fort
date back to the colonial period when the fort was constructed by the
Portuguese in the 16th century and later fortified by the Dutch in the
17th century.

The Sun Bastion within Galle Fort, Sri Lanka, stands as a historic stronghold constructed by the Dutch in the 17th century. Offering scenic views of the Indian Ocean, it remains a symbol of the fort's defensive prowess and colonial heritage, attracting tourists with its architectural charm and panoramic vistas.

Many people come here to have a look at the **Watchtower.**

The Galle Watch Tower, situated in the historic Galle Fort of Sri Lanka, stands as a testament to the region's colonial past. Built by the Dutch in the 17th century, it offers panoramic views of the Indian Ocean and the charming streets of Galle, attracting visitors with its historical significance.

There is also history written in English in nearby places. You can read that and continue your journey. It was raining and I wanted to take some rest and have some coffee too. I started walking outside this fort and found a place to rest and have some coffee at the **Galle fort restaurant .**

I had coffee with this book . I liked this book ,read a few paragraphs and continued my journey towards my guest house . As this was my last day of travel in Galle I have to go back to Colombo to catch the flight on 3rd January . I had my train booked from Galle to Colombo tomorrow morning on 2nd January .

Chapter 11: Day 9, From Galle to Colombo

2nd January , this day will cover my journey from Galle to Colombo and a few sightseeing in Colombo . I felt maybe I missed a few things in Colombo.

I took the last photograph of my guest house at Galle before leaving this place , completed all the formalities given the keys to the owner and thanked him for all the help he has given to me.

I started waiting for my train at Galle station.

I met on the couch surfing app and made a few friends and one of my friends suggested that I should visit **One Galle Face mall** in Colombo.

I checked into the hotel and started my journey towards One Galle Face mall in Colombo.

The grand entrance of the Grand Oriental Hotel in Colombo beckons guests with its timeless charm and elegance. A symbol of luxury and hospitality, it offers a captivating retreat for travelers seeking an unforgettable stay amidst the bustling cityscape of Sri Lanka's vibrant capital.

One Galle Face Mall is a premier shopping destination in Colombo, Sri Lanka. Spanning luxurious retail outlets, dining options, and entertainment facilities, it offers a vibrant experience for visitors. With its modern architecture and upscale amenities, it's a hub for both locals and tourists seeking leisure and indulgence.

There was a new year celebration going on inside the mall and I found myself lucky to see the decoration was still present on the 3rd of January.

In the above image you can see the decorations they have made for the new year. This was made for Christmas day and was still available. Mall was decorated very nicely , the mall was very clean and the ambience at the mall was also great.

I also visited many electronic shops , clothes shops.

The SINGER brand shop in One Galle Face Mall, Colombo, exudes modern sophistication with its sleek design and expansive display of appliances and electronics. From state-of-the-art home appliances to cutting-edge gadgets, it offers a comprehensive shopping experience, embodying SINGER's legacy of quality, innovation, and customer satisfaction.

I had some food inside the mall. There are many food options available here.

Just look at these Potato Spicy balls called Vada Pav in India. You should search for Food studio inside this mall if you want to try various cuisines from different countries here.

The Food Studio is a culinary haven, boasting a diverse array of cuisines from around the globe. With an extensive menu featuring dishes from various countries, it offers a tantalizing journey for food enthusiasts, catering to diverse palates and providing an immersive dining experience rich in flavors and cultural exploration.

As I was walking and roaming inside the mall I found a Colombo coffee company shop inside the mall . I had one espresso here and it was awesome.

You can find various varieties of coffee beans , coffee and coffee equipment here.

After this mall visit I went back nearby to my hotel to meet my couch surfing friend . With my friend I visited the local market and some shops , and purchased a few clothes . I was not able to capture photos of the market as the market was very much crowded.

But my friend took me to a hotel named **Ministry of Crab** and we took this photo here where the chef is showing the big crab . If you are a crab lover you can try some crab dishes here.

I said thanks to my friend and went back to my hotel. 3rd January is my flight back to Chennai early in the morning.

Chapter 12: Day 10, Colombo airport and back to India

3rd January

I reached Colombo airport early around 6 AM with my cab driver.

I took some coffee beans from this shop Rancrisp , you can find this shop at Colombo international airport.

PART 2: Joy's Journeys in Sri Lanka

Chapter 1: Cultural triangle of Sri Lanka

In this chapter, we review a few Buddhist places in Sri Lanka. Sri Lanka is an ancient Buddhist country which has Buddhism for thousands of years. Buddhism was brought here from India by emperor Ashoka's son Mahinda, who planted the sapling from the original Bodhi at Anuradhapura.

Buddhist places in Sri Lanka include the cultural triangle consisting of Anuradhapura, Dambulla, and Polonnaruwa. Kandy, the city of the temple of the tooth, is also an important Buddhist holy city.

Figure: Kandy in central Sri Lanka, site of Sri Dalada Maligawa temple of the tooth

1. How to get to Sri Lanka

Citizens of Indian and many other countries can get visa on arrival or evisa to Sri Lanka. Many European countries and US citizens do not need a visa for short stays.

The easiest way to enter Sri Lanka is to take a flight to Colombo. One can also travel by the newly launched cruise boat service from Tamil Nadu in India.

One can withdraw Sri Lankan rupees at the ATMs in the airport, or else one can change money from INR to LKR at the airport where there are branches of Sri Lankan banks. In columbo markets near Fort, also one can exchange currencies.

1.2 How to get to the cultural triangle

Colombo airport is the main airport in Sri Lanka and is accessible from many major airlines.

From Colombo airport one can either take taxi or bus. There is a direct bus to Kandy from Kerunegela bus stand, which is a very short distance from Colombo airport.

Or else, one can travel from Colombo airport to the main bus stand in Colombo city and take buses to Kandy or Anuradhapura etc from there. One can also take the train from Colombo fort railway station.

Chapter 2: Kandy

In this chapter, we review a few places in Kandy. Kandy city is located in the center of Sri Lanka. It has one of the holiest places in Sri Lanka, a Buddhist temple called temple of the tooth or Sri Dalada Maligawa.

Figure: Entrance to Sri Dalada Maligawa Buddha tooth temple in Kandy

Figure: Inside temple of the tooth Sri Dalada Maligawa in Kandy

Figure: Moat around the temple of the tooth in Kandy

Figure: Decorated moonstone at the temple of the tooth in Kandy

2.1 Sri Dalada Maligawa Buddha tooth temple in Kandy

Sri Dalada Maligawa is the holiest temple in Sri Lanka, since it has the Buddha tooth relic. It is a very living place and one can just sit in peace and observe the mass of humanity offering flowers and the other ceremonies here. The relic is displayed and worshipped once or twice a day. There is also a big festival once a year when the relic is carried in a procession. There are a few museums in the vicinity including the international Buddhist museum, which is also worth seeing.

The Buddha's tooth relics is located in the relic chamber on the first floor. Lots of worshippers were reverently sitting or meditating, offering beautiful lotus flowers and other offerings.

The whole complex has amazing architecture. It also has a dalada museum and an amazing international Buddhist museum. One meditation hall had gifts of thai and burmese and buddha's feet etc, and an exhibition of dalada history, since it was brought from india by two ministers fleeing a war. It was said to give rains where there was drought. There is a legend that whoever owned Dalada ruled Sri Lanka. The tooth relic passed through different capitals including Anuradhapura and Polonnaruwa before coming to the Kandyan kingdom and finally to the british.

Outside the dalada maligawa one has to deposit all bags and also deposit one's shoes. For foreigners entrance in 2019 was 1000 LKR and for SAARC nationals it was 500, however prices are subject to change. There is a thorough security check before entering the complex, since the place was target on an LTTE attack once.

Figure: International Buddhist museum building in Kandy, located close to Sri Dalada Maligawa truth temple complex

2.2 International Buddhist museum in Kandy

The International Buddhist museum is located just next to the Dalada maligawa temple complex. It has entry LKR 500 for foreign nationals. It has a huge Sri lankan Buddhism section, where there were scale models of the various monastery complexes and an overview of history of Buddhism in sri lanka, both theravada and mahayana. There were also statues of avalokiteshwara in Sri lanka. The museum has information about the historical rivalry between the Abhayagiri vs Jetavana monasteries, with Abhaygiri having heretical Mahayana doctrines from india, while Jetavana stuck to Theravada. There was a section of dalada tooth relic and golden casket, also the procession on elephants, and the keeper of the relic, 10 day festival in august beginning, was significant.

The museum also has sections from different Buddhist countries,

- There was the bangadeshi section with ruins of several ancient monasteries found there.

- The Burmese section had the life of a child getting initiated into monkhood as a rite of passage. Also had overview of the shwedagon pagoda, which is built like a mandala. Every layer of that mandala represents a different concept like suffering, buddhas, world of men etc. It also had an overview of pagodas in bagan and so on and the new capital, and a display of a complete burmese shrine with all its components.

- The thai section had a display on the king who is like dharma raja or a bodhisattva, the keeper of dharma. It also had an overview of different ancient moansteries like in bangkok and lanna kingdom, sukothai etc.

- The upper story had the malaysian Buddhism section, telling how since ancient kingdoms of sri vijaya, malaysian monks and lay people are again spreading out and spreading buddhism. It had exhibits related to the sri lankan temple in Malaysia and a temple in chinese style in a malaysian island Penang. It also had a temple with each floor of a different style, base chinese octagon, middle thai and top burmese pagoda.

- The Indonesian section spoke of its history and the amazing temple like a mandala at borobodur, had a scale model too.

- The Vietnam section spoke of hue and hanoi and saigon temples.

- The china section had an interesting part on how a tooth relic was excavated after thousands of years from an underground temple. It had a section of the four sacred

Buddhist hills in China, such as the hill of manjushri Wutai mountain and others. It also spoke of theravada buddhism, such as the gold pagoda, in yunnan province in China. It covered the chinese buddhist association and friendship with sri lanka. Covered the schools of chinese buddhism.

• The Japan section spoke of how it was the pinnacle of all the different buddhist schools where it flourished in most developed form. It had displays of a Japanese monk's bowl, robe, colourful paper lanterns and decorations, images etc. It spoke separately of all the traditions of dogen's zen, the esoteric traditions, the pure land school, nichiren and so on.

• The korean section had a korean shrine and monk's bowl and temple bell, etc.

• There was a huge Indian Buddhism section, with details of different Buddhist monasteries and temples located in India.

2.3 My experience of visiting Kandy in 2015

I took the ETA e-visa (15 US dollars) 2 months in advance from the embassy website, and got a cheap flight on Air India express (About Rs 6500 return) from Chennai to Colombo. Contacted some Sri Lankan friends and did some research on the sacred sites in the meantime. I didnt have much Indian Rupees cash so took along mainly the Euros and other foreign currency I had with me, as well as the credit and debit cards from UK.

On the day of the visit on Friday I took a deluxe bus, Rs 360, 2:40 pm till 11 pm, from Bangalore Shanthinagar bus station to Chennai CMBT bus station, from there got a 70A bus to the airport after much asking. Spent the night at the airport waiting lounge, fortunately got a place to sit. Next morning was the flight.

I arrived in Colombo and exchanged 55 euros for close to 9000 LKR from peoples bank counter at the airport itself. Then just outside the airport I was lucky to get a bus straight going to Kandy (Rs 140 LKR) but had to stand for like 2 out of the 3 hours. I found Sri Lanka very green indeed. It started around 8:50 am and reached close to 11:40. On the way passed through the amazingly beautiful university of Perideniya, nestled among the hills. I was tired and weary. I asked a police officer where is tooth temple, who did not understand my English, but unfortunately a driver named Mahesh understood and offered top 'drop me' there. Not for free, I guess was implied. On the way he tried to get me interested in sex and message, best in Sri Lanka, and cheap accomodation, cheaper than 4000-5000 LKR. He said in Kandy the good places to see are tea museum, tooth temple, palace, botanical gardens, one can buy batik etc. Anyway thankfully he dropped me outside the Dalada maligawa and took LKR 350, over charging but at least he took me there and had some guide tips.

Outside the dalada maligawa one has to deposit all bags (pay a tip like 10 or 20 LKR when collecting) and also inside the complex deposit all shoes. For foreigners entrance was 1000 LKR and for SAARC nationals it was 500. I just got in since I look like a Sri Lankan, so nobody stopped or checked, even though I wasnt wearing white. There was a security check, since the place was target on an LTTE attack once. Inside I went straight up to the relic chamber, a film was running on the golden casket of the tooth. Lots of worshippers were reverently sitting or meditating, offering beautiful lotus flowers too. Later had a look around the complex. Its amazing architecture. It also had a dalada museum (think there was the elephant who always came for the procession, stuffed after he died) and an amazing international Buddhist museum. One meditation hall had gifts of thai and burmese and buddha's feet etc, and an exhibition of dalada history, since it was brought from india by two ministers fleeing a war. It was said to give rains where there was drought, legend was who owned dalada ruled sri lanka. finally it passed through different capitals before coming to the kandyan kingdom and the british.

The Buddhist museum, entry LKR 500 for foreign nationals, had a huge sri lankan section, where there were scale models of the various monastery complexes and an overview of history of buddhism in sri lanka, both theravada and mahayana. I was surprised to see there were also statues of avalokiteshwara in Sri lanka. the abhayagiri vs jetavana rivalry, with abhaygiri having heretical mahayana doctrines from india, was also displayed, which also started a war. There was a section of dalada tooth relic and golden casket, also the procession on elephants, and the keeper of the relic, 10 day festival in august beginning, was significant.

After getting out of the museum went around the city a bit, saw the beautiful kandy lake. sw lots of heritage buildings around city centre. walked to city market near railway stationm, bought some stuff like snacks and chocolates for LKR 231 (bit expensive i thought).

Then i was very tired so saw and went to tourist police building, asked them for help finding accomodation cheap. one friendly guy said it is for LKR 1000-2000 or so non AC, got a tuk tuk and said it will take 150 LKR. the tuk tuk driver drove through the hills around kandy to the guest house, which supposedly had an honest man running it. I was given a room, gave my passport and 2000 cash, had a quick shower, the owner came in, it was around 4 pm. he showed me the map and places to see, sai there is bus tomorrow 6 am leaving to anuradhapura, AC bus. i also had fried rice Rs 350 and chicken Rs 350 plus coke total Rs 830 LKR, bit pricey. But had a nice sleep. the owner showed me many guide books which i read with great enthusiasm, covering whole history of sri lanka buddhism. he suggested go for outhern west beaches, yala national park in south east etc. i slept early around 9 pm after having lunch at 8 pm.

Chapter 3: Anuradhapura

In this chapter, we visit some places in Anuradhapura. Anuradhapura is one of the ancient capitals of Sri Lanka and the oldest of them. It is located to the north of Kandy.

Figure: Sri Maha Bodhi tree in Anuradhapura

3.1 Sri Maha Bodhi tree in Anuradhapura

Sri Maha Bodhi is one of the holiest places in Sri Lanka, after the tooth temple. It is built out of a sapling of the main Bodhi tree in Bodhgaya where the Buddha meditated and became enlightened. Later the original tree was destroyed in India but was re=planted with a sapling of this Sri Lankan Mahabodhi tree.

The Mahabodhi tree has been continuously guarded for over 2000 years, by soldiers, priests etc. Lots of reverent worshippers were there near the tree. I took a circumambulation round of the tree and meditated for a short while. Lots of monkeys were in the area too.

Figure: Signboard showing location of different stupas in Anuradhapura

Figure: Twin pond in Anuradhapura, where the monks went to take a bath

3.2 Monasteries in Anuradhapura

Anuradhapura is the ancient capital of Sri Lanka and peak of the cultural triangle. There are a number of important monasteries there including the following:

- Abhayagiri monastery

- Lankaramaya

- Vessagiri cave complex

- Thuparamaya dagoba

- Ruwanvesaliya

- Jetavana Vihara

Figure: Ancient Abhayagiri stupa in Anuradhapura

3.3 Abhayagiri Monastery complex and stupa

Abhayagiri is the huge ancient mahayana monastery complex. There was a huge circular pond, beautiful moonstones next to it, a historical exhibition in it. Couldnt really circumambulate the monastery since it was so huge.

Figure: Lankarama stupa in Anuradhapura

3.4 Lankaramaya Vihara

This has the design of a nice neat monastery complex with the following components: Lake outside, living quarters (several), administrative quarters, the main stupa, Bodhi tree shrine.

3.5 Vessagiri cave complex

This was a cave complex, where monks used to meditate beneath stones and huge rock boulders. They had cut seats, steps, even water lines in the rocks. I meditated for a few minutes in the same spot. Some of the rocks also had some paintings which were damaged now. Other rocks had some inscriptions in old sinhala. It also had a vantage point where one could see the three big pagodas, sigiriya and other sights. Coming down the stairs we saw the administrative complex for the monks.

3.6 Thuparamaya Dagoba

It was a complete complex, little but also quite beautiful. Some of the parts are still ruins. Crowds of worshippers were offering flowers and circum-ambulating the stupa, and the resident monk was leading a chanting session.

Figure: Ruwanveli maha stupa in Anuradhapura, along with elephant statues

3.7 Ruvanveli stupa and monastic complex

The ruwanweli stupa and monastic complex is huge in size. It is an ancient stupa, built by king Duthugamunu in 4th century AD, huge in size and a living stupa. It is still a very popular place and object of worship, painted white and lots of visitors and worshippers. I managed to circumambulate the huge stupa. There were elephant images all around. also statues of the king and the queen. It was really peaceful, although crowded.

Figure: Jetavana vihara in Anuradhapura

3.8 Jetavana Vihara

This is one of the most ancient viharas and historically very significant. It was of the orthodox sect theravada in rivalry with Abhaya Giri (mahayana) It was huge structure of size comparable to pyramids in giza Egypt, one of the wonders of the ancient world. There was a huge banyan tree outside as well.

3.9 My experience of visiting Anuradhapura in 2015

Sunday morning from Dambulla I took tuk tuk auto at 6 am, to bus station, cost LKR 250. From there found the AC bus, chinese made, to anuradhapura. It was so beautiful the journey, lots of palm trees and green fields and hills and all greenery. It reached around 9:30 am, first old and finally the new bus station. i wandered around a bit to the sunday market opposite new bus station, then made mistake of asking someone and the auto driver pala found me and said only LKR 200 he will get me to bodhi tree. but he was really very nice. he said the normal entry is USD 25, but he can get me around for only LKR 3500, 1500 to bribe the police and 2000 for his charges. i thought its ok. it was 1500 in advance and the rest at the end.

So first we went to vessagiri cave complex where monks used to meditate beneath stones and huge rock boulders. they had cut seats, steps, even water lines in the rocks. i meditated for 2 minutes in the same spot. also had some paintings which were damaged now. had some inscriptions in old sinhala. also had a vantage point where one could see the 3 big pagodas, sigiriya and other sights.

Then we went through a dakkhina stupa, largely ruined, having bones of some saints, a triumphalist stupa being built by rajapaksa and bye army to celebrate his 'victory' over the tamil LTTE. there was also an army canteen where one could get stuff relatively cheaply.

Then we visited the maha bodhi sacred tree. i left shoes at the auto itself as advised wisely. then went via the western gate (entry is free, eastern gate it is LKR 200 entry. it was the maha bodhi tree, continuously guarded for over 2000 years, by soldiers, priests etc. lots of reverent worshippers were there too. i took a round of the tree and meditated for a short while. then went forward to nearby brazen palace, lots of monkeys were in the area too. then came back to pala the auto driver.

Then pala, my Sri Lankan guide, took me to a monastery complex (relatively small, i later came to know, at that time i thought it was quite big!) the main stupa was in white and still was an object of worship. i circumambulated the stupa and took photos.

Then we passed through a lake a huge huge man made lake during time of duttha gamini 2nd century AD. it was beautiful. some cycle racers passed by. one mischievous boy threw water on them. also passed some lotus ponds.

Then we went to the huge ruwan weli stupa. its a popular object of worship, painted white and lots of visitors and worshippers.

circumambulated. there were elephant images all around. also statues of the king and the queen. it was really peaceful, although crowded.

Then we went to a huge load of sites with pala, including the royal palace, 2 pools, several lakes and lotus ponds, huge refectories. i hadnt seen this on such a scale since hampi. but hampi was a baby compared with this ancient capital of 1000 years. went through ruins of an ancient kali temple, some lesser visited shrines.

We also visited the lankaramaya stupa, where there was design of a nice neat monastery complex with the following components:

- Lake outside

- Living quarters (several)

- Administrative quarters

- The main stupa

- Bodhi tree shrine

There was one priest posted in several of the stupas/ dagobas who was telling visitors to chant certain suttas.

Next we came to abhaya giri, the huge ancient mahayana monastery complex. there was a huge circular pond, beautiful moonstones next to it, a historical exhibition in it.

Pala drove through middle of the forest, through the small canals, through shortcuts in very rough area a few streets were being rebuilt for the full moon day poya celebrations. this was off season for tourists, a few months later they will come in droves. saw the main priest's house, which was in pallava style wooden top, 2 floors (out of which only one floor remained). also saw the original temple of the tooth, which moved as the capital of the sinhalaese kings also moved, first to ponnoruwa then finally kandy.

Finally we came to the main stupa, most ancient jetawana vihara. huge structure of size comparable to pyramids in giza Egypt, one of the wonders of the ancient world. there was a huge banyan tree. was amazed at the level of culture of the ancients. saw the 2 ponds, amazing architecture of stairs etc and the system of canals that brought water even in drought filled times.

On the way, Pala told me about his daughter, aged about 14, Rs 2500 per hour for violen classes, he hopes to send her to university some day. he dropped me in front of new bus station. i took AC bus to colombo.

The AC bus charged LKR500 but had a really nice concert Sri lankan traders association, lovely music and dance. we passed through amazing scenery again, its so good to be able to settle here. we stopped at one place and it was raining. passed many small towns and villages. we started on the bus close to 2:30 pm, reached colombo fort in 6 hours at 8:30 pm.

Alas, it was sunday and all was closed. i had hoped to see a bit of colombo also but it wasnt to be. saw there was some dutch museum nearby, but that time in night wasnt possible. lots of hotels were there, serving food and accommodation. just took a walk to colombo market, just like in UK a covered market selling clothes and toys and watches etc, a catholic church, near the railway station. finally took the AC bus to airport, Rs 100 LKR. Had to roam around a lot because there is quite some distance between the bus stop and airport departures, its all rather very confusing. Fortunately they didnt check the departure time. there were total about 5-6 levels of security. as expected, everything in airport was overpriced, i lost quite an amount of money buying teas, chocolates, souvenirs, postcards etc. next day flight was late by 3 hours and i was stuck, still inside everything was to be paid in dollars inside the departure lounge. got some buddhist books and CDs etc. then departed for chennai back on air india express.

Chapter 4: Dambulla

In this chapter, we visit some places in Dambulla, which is part of the cultural triangle. Dambulla is famous for the cave temples with rich painted roofs.

Figure: Exterior of the cave temple in Dambulla, Sri Lanka

Figure: Painting on the wall of Dambulla cave temple in Sri Lanka

4.1 How to get to Dambulla

To get to Dambulla from Columbo airport, one can take a bus from the airport to Kurunegala, and from there one can change to a bus to Dambulla. The cost of a bus ticket is quite minimal, less than 5 USD.

The Dambulla cave complex is a UNESCO world heritage site and has 5 cave temples. It is a short walk or take an auto from the Dambulla bus station.

4.2 Dambulla cave temples

The cave temples consist of amazing rock cut caves full of paintings of the buddha. Some of the caves have low lighting to preserve the paintings. They are possibly influenced by ajanta caves paintings in india and in the same style. There are five caves in total. Entry from golden temple side is on top of hill after climbing more than 350 steps. Be careful to buy the ticket before you begin to climb, since the ticket office at the top may be closed. Separate kings entry steps from car park. Cost for foreigners is 1500 LKR in 2021, but prices may change.

The Dambulla cave temple is on top of a rocky hillock, and can be viewed only after climbing many steps. There are many monkeys during the climb. At the temple itself, the monkeys were kept away via electric wire.

The cave temple is quite unique. There are white decorative entrances built in Portuguese church style, before entering the actual caves.

4.3 Cave temple 1

The first cave temple has buddhas carved out of solid rock.

Figure: Sitting and standing Buddha statues in Dambulla cave temple 2 in Sri Lanka

Figure: Stupa with sitting Buddhas in Dambulla cave temple 2 in Sri Lanka

4.4 Cave temple 2

The second temple is the best of the lot, with the sitting buddhas around the stupa. It is quite huge.

Figure: Statue of the Kandy king along with sitting Buddhas in Dambulla cave temple

4.5 Cave temples 3,4 and 5

The last three cave temples were built later, and are a bit less sophisticated.

One of the temples has the tamil indian king of kandy's image as well, since it was him, one of the last kings of kandy, who renovated that cave temple.

4.6 My experience of seeing the Dambulla cave temples in 2015

The temple is on top of a rocky hillock, after climbing many (tiring) steps.

There were just so many monkeys during the climb! At the temple itself, the monkeys were kept away via electric wire.

The ticket office was in a part I didnt see at the entrance, so had to climb the cave twice its 350 steps, felt a lot lot more and tiring. There were also a lot of monkeys on the steps leading to the caves.

The cave temple is quite unique and strange, built a bit in Portuguese church style (the ones you see in Goa) but being a Buddhist temple nonetheless!

The 5 caves were utterly dark but magnificient. All the buddhas carved no the roof and sides and front of the cave. The 5 caves each have their unique properties. Hindu gods were also there in one cave.

The entry fees to the Dambulla cave temple was LKR 1500 for foreigners.

Chapter 5: Polonnaruwa

In this chapter, we visit some places in Polonnaruwa, which is also part of the cultural triangle and one of the ancient capitals of Sri Lanka. It is newer than Anuradhapura and located to the south of Anuradhapura.

5.1 How to get to Polonnaruwa

One can get a bus to Polonnaruwa from Kandy bus stand.

To travel inside polonnaruwa, one can take a tuk tuk auto. It may cost around 2500 LKR or more for a few hours.

The ticket cost for foreigners is about 30 USD, the price is subject to increase.

There is also a museum in Polonnaruwa close to the historical sites, the museum price is included in the ticket. .

5.2 Temples in Polonnaruwa

Polonnaruwa is one of the ancient capitals of Sri Lanka. The archeological zone in Polonnaruwa has a number of amazing temples including the following temples:

- **Vatadage**

- **Kiri Vihara**

- **Lankatilaka Vihara**

- **Gal Vihara**

Figure: Vatadage in Polonnaruwa

1. Vadatage

The vadatage is simply magnificent in its beauty and symmetry. It is within the sacred quadrangle at Polonnaruwa. It is a circular stupa, largely intact and very well maintained. The moonstone is amazing. It has several buddha statues of sitting buddha. It is one of the highlights of polonnaruwa.

5.4 Kiri Vihara

Kiri Vihara is the only completely intact stupa within the Polonnaruwa ruins. It is in the middle of a huge monastic complex with living quarters, library, meditation room, kitchen etc of the monks.

Figure: Standing Buddha statue in Lankatilaka vihara in Polonnaruwa

1. Lankatilaka Vihara

Lankatilaka is within a complex of ancient temples. It has a huge standing buddha in the centre, and lots of carvings on the walls.

Figure: Sitting Buddha statue in Gal Vihara in Polonnaruwa

Figure: Standing and sleeping Buddha in Gal Vihara in Polonnaruwa

5.6 Gal Vihara

It is one of the most visited and famous places in polonnaruwa.

Gal Vihara has 4 buddhas in different postures: 2 sitting buddhas in meditative posture, one standing buddha and one in sleeping posture.

It also has ancient sinhala inscriptions on a rock face by king Parakramabahu. The whole thing was cut from solid rock, reflecting the skill of the craftsmen.

Figure: Cambodian monk tomb in Polonnaruwa

5.7 My experience of visiting Polonnaruwa with a tour guide in 2021

The guide gave me 2 hour tour.

The entry ticket to Polonnaruwa was 1250 LKR for SAARC citizens, which is 50% off the usual tourist rate which was 2500 LKR in 2021.

We started with the palace burnt by the cholas.

Then we visited the royal chamber whose roof was gone but pillars were there.

After that, we visited the magnificient vadatage and galatage: the tooth relic was kept here.

There was even a chola shiva temple nearby.

Within 100 m from the Chola temple was a famous cambodian monk's tomb, and near to that many other monk tombs.

A few hundred metres from this, there was a white stupa: huge one, 4th biggest in sri lanka. We visited a few such stupas.

Lastly, we visited the gala vihara which had 3 buddhas sitting sleeping and standing: different poses, and rock cut inscription.

There was also a museum detailing the history and artifacts from Polonnaruwa. The museum entry was included in the ticket price.

Then we saw the huge Parakram samudra lake constructed by king Parakram Bahu.

Finally, at the end of the tour, I said goodbye to the guide, paid him 1500 LKR.

Chapter 6: Sigiriya

In this chapter, we visit the great lion rock of Sigiriya. Sigiriya is also part of the cultural triangle and located close to Dambulla.

6.1 How to get to Sigiriya

One can take a bus to Sigiriya from Dambulla bus stand. The bus can be quite crowded and hot in the summer time

One needs to take a ticket to see the Sigiriya historical UNESCO world heritage site. The cost of the ticket is around USD 30 for foreigners and USD 15 for SAARC countries and Indian nationals.

Figure: View of the lion rock at Sigiriya

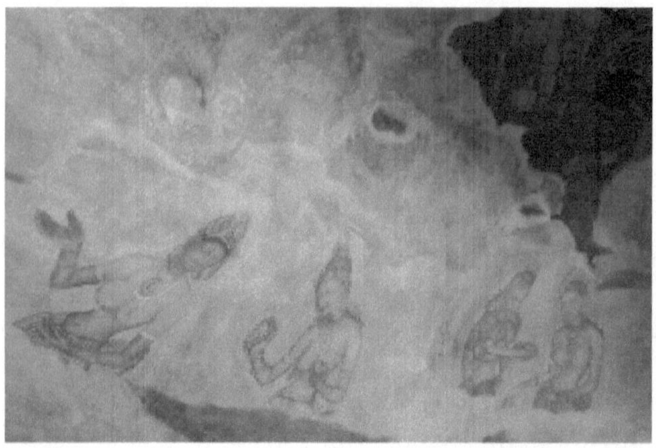

Figure: Paintings on the lion rock at Sigiriya

Figure: Climbing the lion rock at Sigiriya

6.2 Sigiriya lion rock

The rock palace is a palace built in 5th century by king kassapa, being scared of a relative and rival who would later invade with an army and kill him. It is a palace built on top of a solid rock face. There are a number of cave temples on parts of the rock face. Perhaps the rock has a long history behind it.

It takes at least 3 hours for a traveler to climb the stairs and reach the top and back down again.

6.3 My experience of climbing the Sigiriya lion rock in 2015

Climbing the Sigiriya lion rock was for me very tiring and took a long time. It took around 1.5 to 2 hours to climb it. Climbing down was shorter time, less than an hour. I did not take any tour guide and climbed by myself.

The rock palace is a palace built in 5th century by king kassapa, being scared of a relative and rival who would later invade with an army and kill him. It is a palace built on top of a solid rock face.

There are a number of cave temples on parts of the rock face. Perhaps the rock has a long history behind it.

I started climbing the rock by 10 am and finished by 1 pm.

The cost was 3000 LKR for westerner foreigner and half price ie 1500 LKR for SAARC passport holders.

www.ingramcontent.com/pod-product-compliance
Lightning Source LLC
Chambersburg PA
CBHW021945120726
47992CB00001B/158